YO-CXN-283

Rodrigo and the DOGS

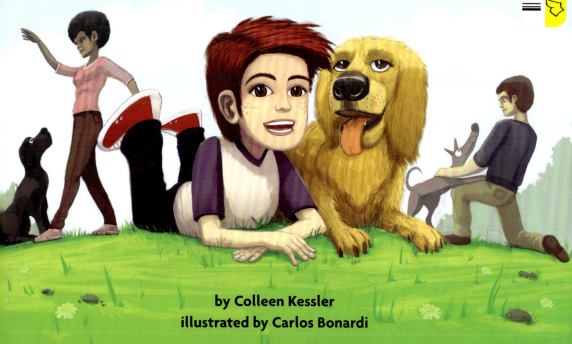

by Colleen Kessler
illustrated by Carlos Bonardi

Table of Contents

"Rodrigo, where are you? It's time to get going."

"I'm out here, *Mami*," Rodrigo called from the yard, not lifting his head from the die-cast metal soldiers he was carefully arranging into position for the next battle. He was recreating the First Battle of Bull Run, a pivotal event from the early part of the Civil War. Rodrigo loved orchestrating these skirmishes—all the noise and action of the battlefield—and running the **maneuvers**. "Prepare to take cover behind the barn, men," he said in his most commanding voice as he moved five infantry pieces along the path he'd laid out earlier. "Keep an eye out for those Yanks, Sergeant Santo," he instructed the old golden retriever, lying in the shade, well beyond his theater of operations.

"Come inside. We have to leave to visit your **abuelo**," his mother reminded him from the doorway.

abuelo Spanish for "grandfather"

"Just a minute," Rodrigo answered as he positioned the soldiers on top of the pebble structure he had designated the barn. "Here we go; it's time to spring our trap," he whispered. As Rodrigo began making shooting noises, Santo, the golden retriever, abandoned his sentry position and came running, severely **decimating** the enemy troops as he spun in excited circles. Rodrigo fell over laughing; his canine attack strategy worked every time!

Mrs. Ramirez came outside, hands on her hips. "I am not going to ask you again. **Vámanos**! It's time to come inside."

"Okay, okay. We're coming." He knew he couldn't test his mom's patience any further.

On Saturday afternoons, Rodrigo visited his abuelo at the **rehabilitation center**, where he was recovering from hip surgery. His grandfather was doing well, but it would take some time for him to walk well enough to return home.

Vámanos Spanish for "Let's go!"
rehabilitation center a place where people stay to recover from surgery or an injury

After his mom dropped him off at Woodhaven, the rehabilitation center and assisted-living facility, Rodrigo found his abuelo in the recreation room. He was sitting at a table with a few residents, absorbed in a card game. Rodrigo assumed they were playing poker or blackjack, but as he approached the group, someone called out, "Go fish!"

"Hi, Abuelo," Rodrigo said as he kissed the old man on the forehead.

"Ah, Rodrigo, *mi nieto*." His grandfather smiled at him. "I was wondering when you would get here. Sit. We were just starting a new game; my friend Alden here can deal you in."

"Sure," Rodrigo said, sliding into an empty chair.

"So, tell me, what have you been up to? Are you taking good care of Santo?"

"Of course I am. He sleeps on my bed, although Mami doesn't like that. But I tell her that's what you always did with Santo."

mi nieto Spanish for "my grandson"

His grandfather chuckled. "You're right; he did sleep on my bed. I have to spoil my baby, you know; he's the only one I have now that your grandmother is gone and your mom is all grown up."

Abuelo looked down at his cards, and Rodrigo noticed a **melancholy** look spread across his face.

"Santo sure was spoiled by your king-size bed," he said, trying to lighten the mood. "In my little bed, he's squished. In the middle of the night, he rolls over, and on more than a few occasions, I've woken up on the floor while he's **sprawled** out on his back, looking very comfortable and quite content."

Everyone at the card table laughed as they pictured Rodrigo peering up from the floor at the big dog very pleased to have taken over the bed.

"I had a sweet little cocker spaniel for years," Alden chimed in wistfully. "Her name was Daisy; my Elizabeth named her after her favorite flower."

"I had two dogs," one of the long-term residents, a man named Franklin, said. "Two beautiful greyhounds—I gave them to my daughter last year when I moved in here."

"That must have been hard," Abuelo said. "It's too bad we can't have our dogs here with us."

The men **reminisced** about their pets as they continued playing the game. All of them had funny stories about the mischief the animals had gotten into, from Daisy pulling up Elizabeth's entire bed of actual daisies to Franklin's greyhounds stealing his socks from the laundry and hiding them in their box of toys.

Rodrigo listened and watched the men's faces light up with their memories. Like Abuelo, he also thought it was a shame that the dogs couldn't live in the facility, but he knew the staff couldn't take care of pets in addition to the patients.

"How was your afternoon with Abuelo?" Rodrigo's mom asked as they finished eating their supper of *carne asada*, rice, and *pico de gallo*.

Rodrigo began telling his mom the tales the residents had shared about their pets. "The stories were funny, but kind of sad, too. You could tell the guys really feel the absence of their dogs. I think Abuelo is lonely without Santo, and I bet you miss your pop, too, huh, Santo?" Rodrigo said as he scratched the golden retriever behind the ears.

Santo cocked his head as if listening to the question, and then licked Rodrigo's hand and nuzzled his head against it.

"I'll take that as a yes," he said, noticing the yearning in the dog's eyes.

carne asada Spanish for "roasted meat"
pico de gallo a Spanish dish that is a spicy salsa made from tomato, onion, and chilies

"What do you think, Mami? Do you think dogs can feel emotions?"

Mrs. Ramirez looked from her son's face to the dog's and couldn't help but notice the sadness in each. "Yes; I do think animals can feel emotions," she answered carefully. "They get attached to people and can sense when something is wrong. I suspect you're right that Abuelo and Santo are missing each other. But they'll be back together once Abuelo finishes his therapy. The others there, who can no longer have their dogs, won't be as fortunate."

"Well, I have an idea how we might be able to make the residents less lonely. But I'm going to need some help." Rodrigo began to explain the plan he had come up with earlier that afternoon.

At the therapy dog training center the next afternoon, Rodrigo stood next to his mom, tapping his foot nervously as he watched Mrs. Brown with Santo. He had met Mrs. Brown a few months earlier at the library when she was doing a "Paws for Reading" program. The German shepherd had been surprisingly calm, even after a couple of little kids screamed when they first saw the big dog. By the end of that session, all of the children, even the ones who had been hiding behind their caregivers at first, were totally at ease petting the animal or reading aloud with it at their side.

Slowly, Rodrigo took a deep breath and asked, "What do you think, Mrs. Brown? Is Santo a candidate for therapy dog training?"

"You were right in your assessment of Santo's **temperament**. I think he could be a wonderful therapy dog, but it's not easy, especially for an older dog. The program takes several weeks, even months, of hard work, for the dog and you. You'll have to work with him at the training center almost every day."

Rodrigo was not about to let her words of caution stand in his way. He was so excited he wanted to jump up and down, but instead, he calmly turned to his mom and politely asked, "May I, Mami?"

Mrs. Ramirez looked to Mrs. Brown, who nodded encouragingly, then down at Santo, whose eyes seemed to be pleading for her to say yes, too.

"Of course you may work with Mrs. Brown, Rodrigo. It's a great idea and your abuelo will be thrilled."

"Thanks, Mami!" Rodrigo said, beaming. "When can we start?"

Mrs. Brown smiled at Rodrigo's enthusiasm. "Actually, you can start right now if you have time; come into the exhibition ring."

Rodrigo followed her into the arena, a cleared area in the center of the room. He lead Santo on his new six-foot leather leash. All around him were dogs sitting, standing, and sniffing one another in greeting.

Mrs. Brown pointed to an open area where Rodrigo could stand with Santo and then moved to the center of the ring to instruct the group. Clapping her hands, she indicated that the class was beginning.

"Good morning every—"

"Woof, woof!" A young black Labrador retriever across from Rodrigo interrupted the session. Santo interpreted the woofing as an invitation to play. He leaped to his feet and lunged across the arena until he reached the end of the leash and was forced to stop. Rodrigo was **mortified**; this was some beginning to his grand plan!

"Santo, come here," he muttered between clenched teeth.

Mrs. Brown walked over to Gus, the black Labrador, and moved her hand toward the dog as she said firmly, "Sit, Gus."

The dog sat right down. Santo had also stopped straining at the end of the leash, much to Rodrigo's relief.

"Good boy," Mrs. Brown cooed as she petted Gus. "Now, although all of your dogs have had some training, we are going to give Santo here a demonstration and start with a basic obedience refresher," she explained, turning back to the group. "Today we will go over how to instruct your dog to sit, get down, stay, and walk on a loose leash." As Mrs. Brown went over each of the basic voice and hand commands, she stressed that the trainers must be firm but also reward the dogs with a treat when they performed correctly.

After the demonstration, the trainers gave their dogs treats. Santo, seeing and smelling the treats, wanted one and barked until Rodrigo, red with embarrassment, asked Mrs. Brown for one.

Mrs. Brown eyed the barking golden retriever, then mumbled, "Old dogs . . . new tricks," before she relented and handed the boy a biscuit.

Chapter 3

The next Saturday, as he was leaving the rehabilitation center after visiting Abuelo, Rodrigo ran into Mr. Thompson, the center's director, outside his office. Rodrigo's mom had already spoken to him about Santo's training as a therapy dog and had gotten permission for Rodrigo to bring the dog to visit once he was certified.

"Oh hi, Mr. Thompson. Thank you so much for agreeing to let Santo come visit my grandfather. I'm Rodrigo, Juan Ramirez's grandson," he blurted out.

"Nice to meet you, Rodrigo. Come in, have a seat. As I told your mom, as long as the dog has passed his examination, our board has no problem with his coming here." Then he smiled. "And your grandfather will be thrilled, too."

Rodrigo nodded his head in agreement and continued nervously. "Well, Mr. Thompson, I was thinking that if being with his dog would help Abuelo recover, maybe others would benefit from seeing animals. So I was wondering—if you are okay with it, of course—if I could check with the training center about organizing a therapy dog program for all of the residents."

"Therapy dogs? That's a neat idea, and an admirable one, too, but we've pretty much maxed out our budget this year. I'm not sure that the board will authorize a new program." Mr. Thompson rubbed his head as if trying to solve a puzzle. After a few long seconds, he sighed and said, "Tell you what, Rodrigo, why don't you ask Mrs. Brown what it would **entail** and let's see what we can do. Okay?"

"Sure, Mr. Thompson! I'll get right back to you," Rodrigo enthused.

"That's great, son. Enthusiasm is the handmaiden of diligence. But a word of caution: a lot of things will have to go right if we are going to start a therapy dog program."

Rodrigo found out what Mr. Thompson meant about enthusiasm and diligence during that night's session with Santo.

"Stay, Santo, stay," Rodrigo commanded, using the flat palm movement he had learned in class. His homework assignment was to practice having Santo stay for at least one full minute. Thus far, the dog had managed thirty seconds at best before he would get up and move away from the towel that marked his "stay" spot.

The training was turning out to be harder than he had imagined. Rodrigo had never liked doing the same thing over and over, but it was clear that repetition and patience were required.

"Okay, free!" Rodrigo offered Santo a treat after releasing the dog. Then he started the process again with the gesture and voice command, and a sigh.

Rodrigo had to admit he was feeling a bit down about the whole project, and not just because Santo was not proving to be the best pupil. Mr. Thompson had gotten the okay from the board to proceed but no funds to support it. Mrs. Brown agreed that it was a worthy cause, yet as a nonprofit, her center didn't have the manpower or resources to contribute **pro bono**. What was Rodrigo going to do? It was a worthy cause, so maybe they could organize a bake sale or a rummage sale and also ask people for donations to support the program.

Patience, Rodrigo, patience, he said to himself. Then, "Oh, free, Santo, free!" He realized with a start that Santo had been sitting quietly the entire time he'd been lost in thought. "Wow, you stayed for at least two minutes. Good job!"

pro bono for free; usually applies to professional services

The training arena looked different today. There was a desk and a chair, a couple of wheelchairs, and several other contraptions Rodrigo didn't know the names of. He realized it must be the beginning of **acclimating** the dogs to the hospital environment.

"I'd like you to walk your dogs around on a loose leash," Mrs. Brown instructed. "Several of our counselors will be impersonating patients and will be wheeling and walking among you with IV poles and various types of walkers. Your job is to keep your charges relaxed, focused on you, and ignoring the hubbub around them." They were also supposed to stop at the desk and talk with the person there to **simulate** the experience of checking in at reception.

By now, Santo and Rodrigo were used to being among the dogs and handlers, but having the trainers impersonating patients was weird. They were trying to make it as realistic as possible, but to Rodrigo it almost felt as if there were a bunch of zombies invading their ring; their movements were so slow.

As one of the "patients" with an IV pole walked by, Santo got tangled up in the tubing that was dragging on the floor. The "patient" immediately stopped moving, looking to Rodrigo for help.

"Sir, if you can stop a minute, I'll disentangle my dog," Rodrigo said as he knelt. "Good, Santo. We'll have to keep an eye out to avoid that tubing, eh boy?"

By now, the dog had learned to not bark, so he wagged his tail in agreement.

When the session ended, Mrs. Brown gathered the group.

"You all came to this course because you want to help

others," Mrs. Brown said as she presented Rodrigo's idea about a rummage sale to raise money to launch the dog therapy program at Woodhaven. Then she added, "To explain the logistics about staging the fund-raiser, here's the great mind behind the idea, Rodrigo Ramirez."

"Thank you, Mrs. Brown," said Rodrigo, a bit self-conscious. "We were thinking we'd have the rummage sale right here at the training center, in two weeks, just after the certification evaluations," he explained. "It's not a lot of time, I know, so it would be great if some of you would like to help out." Rodrigo looked at the group plaintively, wondering if any adults would join a kid's project.

Much to Rodrigo's relief, all of the therapy dog volunteers were excited about donating items they'd been meaning to clear out of their closets. Gus's owner, Lydia, offered to put up signs around town about the sale. Henry, a retired journalist, agreed to contact the local news media to see about running a story about the fund-raiser. And several trainers offered to set up display tables on the day of the sale. There were many more details to attend to, but Rodrigo was delighted with the progress they had made in such a short time.

Now, all Rodrigo had to do was make sure Santo passed the test.

Chapter 5

The morning of the examination, Rodrigo woke up long before his alarm rang. He had that giddy feeling you get when you're both nervous and excited. After a slow start, Santo had done really well with the training, but Rodrigo still worried about how he would perform in front of others. Every reaction and behavior counted toward his score on the evaluation; if Santo didn't get enough points, he wouldn't be able to be a therapy dog.

Abuelo would get past it, but Rodrigo was worried about the other residents and the future of the program. Santo was kind of the mascot.

"Good luck, Rodrigo and Santo," Mami cheered once they arrived at the center.

They aced the first test, where Santo had to pretend to check in at the hospital and then sit calmly while the evaluator inspected him. Then he was perfect waiting with another handler and staying down with other dogs around.

Finally, the only task remaining was the "Testing of Reactions to Unusual Situations." Rodrigo had to walk Santo, have him sit, lie down, get back up, and walk again, all while disorienting things were going on around him, none of which Rodrigo had any clue about.

He clutched Santo's leash anxiously as they went down the hall together. Then, just as they were reaching the initial turn, a young guy ran through the hall, yelling and pushing a cart in front of him. Santo ignored him, and focused solely on Rodrigo. "Good boy," he whispered encouragingly, breathing a sigh of relief.

At the next corner, they reached the point to sit; just as Santo sat back on his haunches, Rodrigo was startled by the loud crash of a metal pan hitting the floor. He held tight to the leash and the dog stayed seated. Rodrigo praised him again, and they continued with the test.

"Hey, doggy, come here," said a "patient" sitting in a wheelchair that seemed to come out of nowhere.

Rodrigo closed his eyes, certain that this was where Santo would slip up. He was such a friendly dog that he had a difficult time ignoring people who wanted to play with him. But Santo just looked up at Rodrigo, sentry-like, waiting for a command from his superior officer. Rodrigo did not give a signal to go, so Santo stayed at his post.

After another ten minutes and three more distractions, they had completed the examination.

Later that day, after all the dogs had taken their final exams, Mrs. Brown announced that their entire group had passed with extremely high scores. The newest class of graduates erupted in cheers, joined by a dozen yipping and barking dogs.

When the **pandemonium** finally quieted down, she continued, "Congratulations! Please come up and receive your official therapy dog certificates."

The following Saturday, Rodrigo stood in the parking lot of the training center making last-minute adjustments to a display of clothes on a folding table. Santo sat next to him wearing his new therapy dog vest.

Nearby, Mrs. Brown arranged handbags on a wire rack. "You have pulled everything together beautifully, Rodrigo. Are you aware we've already received over $500 in donations?"

"Wow! And look at all these people who are here already."

A woman accompanied by a cameraman walked up and asked, "Excuse me, are you Rodrigo Ramirez?"

"Yes, can I help you?" the boy asked, trying to sound professional.

"I'm Rebecca Cassidy from the Channel 16 Noon News."

"Yes, I know, I recognize you from TV," he said, immediately wishing he had said something more intelligent.

"Well, Henry told me about your project, and I was hoping we could get some footage for our show."

"Sure, that would be amazing!" Rodrigo couldn't believe he was actually going to be on TV! More people would definitely come to the sale now.

The live news report must have helped because the rummage sale grew more crowded throughout the afternoon. Rodrigo finally was able to sit down at 5:00 p.m., when he and Mrs. Brown began counting the money they'd raised.

When they had tallied every last coin and check, Mrs. Brown showed him the figure. Rodrigo couldn't believe it. He raised his arms in the air and cheered; they had raised enough money for the program to run for at least a year! Eventually, Rodrigo would have to come up with a way to raise more money, but this was a great start. He couldn't wait to see the look on Abuelo's face when he saw Santo at the center.

Chapter 6

Mr. Thompson had announced there would be a surprise program that Wednesday afternoon, and all the permanent and part-time residents were gathered in the recreation room. After reminding everyone about some other upcoming events, he said, "And now, we have a special guest who will tell you more about this afternoon's activities."

Rodrigo, who was waiting in the hallway with several other handlers and their charges, grasped Santo's leash and walked into the room. Right away, he saw his abuelo sitting in the front row. Abuelo looked down at Santo and stared at the dog's vest. At first he looked confused, but then he seemed to understand what was happening. Tears filled his eyes as Rodrigo took the microphone from Mr. Thompson.

"Hello, everyone," Rodrigo said. "You know my grandfather, Juan Ramirez"—he pointed toward his abuelo—"and no doubt he's told you stories about his dog, Santo. When Abuelo came to the center, both he and Santo were missing each other, so I wanted to find a way they could see each other. Regular pets aren't allowed here, so for the past few months Santo has been training to become a certified therapy dog. Now, both of us can come here! Santo also has some friends who will be joining us. Every Wednesday afternoon, starting today, we will be running a therapy dog program at Woodhaven."

Rodrigo waved to the group of handlers outside, and they entered the room with their dogs. "Please feel free to visit with and pet the dogs; they are here for you," he announced. The room burst into rousing applause.

Alden shouted, "I get the cocker spaniel!" and motioned to the woman with a small cocker spaniel at her side.

Lydia and Gus walked toward an older woman who seemed to perk up at the sight of the black Labrador retriever.

"Buckley?" she said, a faint smile curling upward.

"Um, this is Gus," said Lydia. "You can pet him if you like."

Meanwhile, a beaming Rodrigo made his way to his grandfather, who grabbed him in a big hug.

"*Gracias*, mi nieto, gracias." Abuelo let go of Rodrigo and turned to Santo. "It's good to see you, *mi perro*," he said, stroking the dog's fur happily.

Santo sat right next to Abuelo, turning his head every once in a while to lick his hand. Rodrigo could have sworn the dog had as big a grin on his face as he did.

gracias Spanish for "thank you"
mi perro Spanish for "my dog"

Three months later, Rodrigo and Santo sat in the entry area of Woodhaven, waiting for Abuelo to finish his physical therapy sessions. He was now living at home with Rodrigo's family, but they came to the center each week for the therapy dog program, and then Abuelo would spend thirty minutes lifting weights and doing stretches.

Mr. Thompson stuck his head into the physical therapy room and asked Rodrigo to come into his office.

"Is everything okay, Mr. Thompson?" He hoped there wasn't a problem. It seemed as though the residents loved the program, and he knew that all the dogs always behaved themselves.

"Yes, Rodrigo; everything's fine, but there is someone here who would like to speak with you."

Rodrigo was surprised to see Rebecca Cassidy, the news reporter from the day of the rummage sale, sitting in the director's office.

"Hi, again," she said, holding out her hand.

"It's nice to see you," Rodrigo replied as they shook hands. "Are you planning to do another story about the dog therapy program?"

"No, I'm here for a personal reason. My mother, Ruth, is one of the residents here. I'm not sure if you ever met her because she has Alzheimer's and sometimes stays in her room by herself. But since your program started, she is the happiest she has been in a long time. That black Labrador, Gus, reminds her of our family dog growing up, and she just raves about how wonderful he is."

Rebecca paused, wiping a tear from her face, then continued. "When my mom is with Gus, she has, well . . . it brings back memories of good times that she seemed to have forgotten. And when I visit with her then, it's like it used to be, and . . . "

"Really, Rodrigo," interrupted Mr. Thompson judiciously, "we can't thank you enough for starting this program. I have heard so many stories like Rebecca's. All of the residents are so thrilled to have the dogs visiting them. You have made such a difference for so many people that the board would like to fund the program into the foreseeable future."

"That is fantastic news Mr. Thompson." Rodrigo smiled proudly. "I'm so happy I could help. At first, all I wanted to do was cheer up my abuelo, but now I'm glad that it has turned into so much more."

GLOSSARY

acclimating (A-klih-may-ting) *verb* getting used to new conditions (page 17)

decimating (DEH-sih-may-ting) *verb* reducing by a large number (page 3)

entail (in-TALE) *verb* involve as a necessary part of something (page 14)

maneuvers (muh-NOO-verz) *noun* planned movements of soldiers or ships (page 2)

melancholy (MEH-lun-kah-lee) *adjective* gloomy; sad (page 5)

mortified (MOR-tih-fide) *adjective* filled with shame and embarrassment (page 11)

pandemonium (pan-duh-MOH-nee-um) *noun* disorder and uproar (page 22)

reminisced (reh-mih-NIST) *verb* remembered with fondness (page 6)

simulate (SIM-yuh-late) *verb* duplicate the conditions of something as a way of training (page 17)

sprawled (SPRAWLD) *verb* lay in a relaxed way with the body spread out (page 5)

temperament (TEM-per-ment) *noun* personality as reflected in behavior (page 10)

ANALYZE THE TEXT

Questions for Close Reading

Use facts and details from the text to support your answers to the following questions.

- Why do you think Rodrigo wanted to ensure that all of the residents could benefit from the therapy dogs?

- What is the main idea of this story? Summarize the key details that support your answer.

- What lessons does Rodrigo learn from his experiences?

- Why do you think the author included Chapter 6 in this story?

Comprehension: Analyze Story Elements

Good readers examine the literary elements in a story—its characters, setting, and plot—to develop a better understanding of the work. Write three adjectives to describe Rodrigo. Then provide one example from the story to support each adjective you choose. Use a chart like the one below to help organize your answer.

Adjective	Example